THE LEARNING

Weston I

W9-CPE-742

WORKING IN
WRITING

by Alexis Burling

12 STORY LIBRARY

www.12StoryLibrary.com

Copyright © 2018 by 12-Story Library, Mankato, MN 56003. All rights reserved. No part of this book may be reproduced or utilized in any form or by any means without written permission from the publisher.

12-Story Library is an imprint of Bookstaves and Press Room Editions

Produced for 12-Story Library by Red Line Editorial

Photograph ©: shapecharge/iStockphoto, cover, 1; Yeko Photo Studio/Shutterstock Images, 4; Debby Wong/Shutterstock Images, 5, 21; jacoblund/iStockphoto, 6, 28; Everett Collection/Shutterstock Images, 7; Julie Clopper/Shutterstock Images, 8; Cora Reed/Shutterstock Images, 9, 29; s_bukley/Shutterstock Images, 10; Lionel Urman/SIPA/AP Images, 11; mrpolyonymous CC2.0, 12; Jannis Tobias Werner/Shutterstock Images, 13; dean bertoncelj/Shutterstock Images, 14; Jonathan Weiss/Shutterstock Images, 15; Ognjen1234/Shutterstock Images, 16; Featureflash Photo Agency/Shutterstock Images, 17, 25, 27; BeeBright/Shutterstock Images, 18; PeopleImages/iStockphoto, 19; Brian Maudsley/Shutterstock Images, 20; Marcio Jose Bastos Silva/Shutterstock Images, 22; samchills CC2.0, 23; U.S. Fish and Wildlife Service, 24; elenaleonova/iStockphoto, 26

Library of Congress Cataloging-in-Publication Data
A catalog record for this book is available from the Library of Congress
978-1-63235-451-8 (hardcover)
978-1-63235-518-8 (paperback)
978-1-62143-570-9 (ebook)

Printed in the United States of America
022017

Access free, up-to-date content on this topic plus a full digital version of this book. Scan the QR code on page 31 or use your school's login at 12StoryLibrary.com.

Table of Contents

Who Are Writers?

Many people dream of becoming a writer. In fact, more than 80 percent of Americans think they should write a book. But there's more to writing than just books. There are many different types of writers. Some write fiction, such as mysteries or historical novels. Others travel around the globe and write about real-world events for newspapers.

Still others write the words for advertisements. Their work shows up in magazines and on billboards.

Unlike many other jobs, writers can work just about anywhere. Thanks to the Internet and Wi-Fi, an office isn't always needed. With a laptop computer or tablet, writers can work from home, in restaurants, or even on the beach.

Sometimes a writer's work is published in print, as in books or newspaper articles. Oftentimes, it is published online in blog posts or magazine articles. Sometimes a writer's work is performed in public.

Readers often dream of becoming writers.

For example, playwrights write scripts for actors to read aloud in a play. Whether they work for themselves or for a company, writers are a central part of today's workforce.

Lin-Manuel Miranda wrote the hit Broadway musical *Hamilton*.

THE DIAMOND SUTRA

The printing press was invented in Germany in the mid-1400s. But the world's first printed book was made much earlier. The Chinese printed books by carving letters into blocks of wood and smothering the wood with ink. Then they pressed paper on top to create pages. In 1907, a Buddhist text called *The Diamond Sutra* was found sealed inside a cave near Dunhuang, China. This printed book was created in 868 CE.

43,380
Estimated number of writers in the United States.

- Writers' work can be found in print or online.
- There are many types of writers, from journalists to book authors.
- The Internet allows writers to work in different locations, even at home.

Do Writers Need Degrees?

Learning how to write takes time, energy, and patience. But there are many paths to take in order to obtain those skills. The first step is to read a lot. It is best to read many different genres. Well-written books show how to create a thrilling plot or describe a historical event.

Beginning writers need to pay attention during English classes in high school. These courses help writers improve their vocabularies and learn about sentence structure and grammar. Some writers work on the school newspaper. Many writers attend college. Some even go to graduate schools to earn advanced degrees in writing.

But becoming a successful writer does not always mean a lot of years in school. Getting a job at a magazine or book publisher is a great way to gain

Some writers learn best by studying other books.

THINK ABOUT IT

Which path do you think is most effective for becoming a successful writer: graduate school or a job in publishing? What are the benefits and drawbacks of each?

experience. Many companies have internships for people first starting out. These temporary positions teach newcomers basic skills in the field.

One way to become a better writer is to write more often. Writers do not need special tools to practice their skills. A pencil and paper are all that is needed.

Kurt Vonnegut taught at the Iowa Writers' Workshop for two years.

20,000
Estimated number of yearly applicants for 3,000–4,000 spots in graduate creative writing programs.

- Reading books is a great way to learn how to write.
- Some writers study English or writing in college or graduate school.
- Internships help new writers gain on-the-job experience.
- Writing regularly is essential.

IOWA WRITERS' WORKSHOP

The University of Iowa has the oldest creative writing graduate program in the country. In some years, as many as 1,300 students applied to get in. There are only 50 spots available, split between fiction writers and poets. Students attend classes for two years. Many get publishing deals when they graduate. Famous writers who have attended or taught there include Robert Frost, Kurt Vonnegut, and ZZ Packer.

Who Works on a Fiction Book?

Books can be divided into nonfiction and fiction categories. When it comes to fiction, writers can choose from many different genres, such as science fiction or romance. Madeleine L'Engle became a kids' favorite as soon as she wrote *A Wrinkle in Time*. Walter Dean Myers and Matt de la Peña both won prizes for their young adult novels.

Theodor Seuss Geisel, better known as Dr. Seuss, illustrated many of the books he wrote.

Some writers prefer working on short stories. If a writer is also a talented artist, he or she can create picture books or graphic novels. More often, however, authors team up with illustrators who tell the visual side of stories.

After an author finishes a final manuscript, there is more work to be done. Authors collaborate with lots of people to publish their books. Copyeditors read over the story to make sure there aren't any spelling errors. Typesetters lay out the text on each page. Designers create attention-grabbing covers.

After a book is published, an author's job still is not over.

One fish two fish red fish blue fish   Dr. Seuss

I can Read with My Eyes Shut!   Dr. Seuss

THE CAT IN THE HAT Dr. Seuss

THE CAT IN THE HAT COMES BACK   Dr. Seuss   B-2

Fox in Socks   By Dr. Seuss

Green Eggs and Ham   Dr. Seuss   D-16

Publicists set up this book signing for author Neil Gaiman in Denver, Colorado.

Publicists set up interviews with members of the media. Some authors even go on tour to different cities. They meet fans, speak at schools, and sign books at bookstores.

JACQUELINE WOODSON

Jacqueline Woodson has written more than 30 books for children and adults. In 2014, her memoir about her childhood, *Brown Girl Dreaming*, won a top prize called the National Book Award. Woodson also writes poetry. She became the Young People's Poet Laureate in 2015. She received $25,000 for the honor. Woodson advises young writers to tell their own stories.

100

Estimated number of children's books Walter Dean Myers wrote in his lifetime.

- Most fiction authors choose to write in a specific genre.
- Some authors write short stories or picture books.
- Authors work with illustrators, copyeditors, typesetters, and designers to publish a book.
- Tours help authors meet fans and sell books.

What Does a Journalist Do?

Journalists usually focus on one subject area, called a beat. For example, Christiane Amanpour is an anchor for CNN and reports on global issues. Bob Woodward writes articles and books about politics. Other journalists write about celebrities or environmental concerns.

Journalists typically have to do their own research. Some write articles about people or happenings in their hometowns. Others get paid to travel the world and examine different cultures or events. Before writing a story, journalists interview people over the phone or in person to gather information and quotes.

Since the 1990s, journalism has changed as a career path. In the past, most journalists earned advanced degrees in school. News articles were printed in newspapers or magazines, or read aloud by news anchors. But today, more reporting is published online. Anyone, even kids, can create blogs to describe

Christiane Amanpour has won numerous awards during her journalism career.

Ta-Nehisi Coates is a journalist for *The Atlantic* magazine.

NINE-YEAR-OLD LANDS BOOK DEAL

Hilde Lysiak's father was a reporter at the *New York Daily News*. His job inspired Hilde to start her own newspaper, the *Orange Street News*, when she was seven. Two years later, Hilde wrote an article about a murder in her Pennsylvania hometown. It got the national media's attention. In June 2016, Scholastic asked Hilde to write four books about her investigative adventures.

what's going on around them.

Social media plays a growing role in how journalism is changing, too. Reporters somctimes use social media to find information or inspiration for an article. They also use social media sites to spread their stories to a wider audience.

62
Percent of adults in the United States who get their news using social media.

- Journalists specialize in one subject area, such as politics or news.
- They get paid to travel and report information.
- More journalism is appearing online.
- Social media is a key research tool for journalists.

What's in a Writer's Toolkit?

Computers make it easy to edit and correct mistakes while writing. Resources such as dictionaries and thesauruses are helpful for finding the perfect words to use in a sentence. Writers also have more specialized books in their toolkits. These how-to manuals explain the standards of specialized fields.

William Strunk and E. B. White's *The Elements of Style* is an English style guide that was first published in 1959. It discusses grammar and style choices. The book also lists commonly misused words and expressions. It shows users how to write a strong essay or create a well-structured story.

Other style guides are important when writing for different types of publications. Most newspapers and magazines use the *Associated Press*

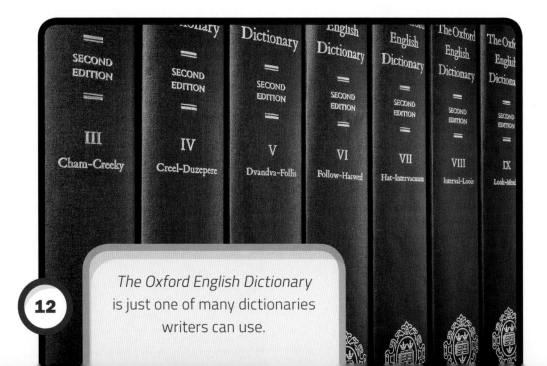

The Oxford English Dictionary is just one of many dictionaries writers can use.

The University of Chicago produced the first *Chicago Manual of Style* more than 100 years ago.

Stylebook. Novelists and nonfiction authors use the *Chicago Manual of Style*. When writing for the medical industry, writers use the style guide made by the American Medical Association. It is called the *AMA Manual of Style*. The *MLA Handbook* is typically used by academic scholars. It is produced by the Modern Language Association.

One of the most popular reference manuals is *Writer's Market*. It contains lists of publishers, editors, and literary agents. Writers use it to search for companies or publications that might want to publish their books or stories.

10 million

Number of copies of *The Elements of Style* sold by the time the book turned 50 in 2009.

- Writers use stylebooks when writing for different types of publications.
- Stylebooks instruct users on grammar and how to write.
- *Writer's Market* gives advice on how to get published.

How Do Writers Make a Living?

Can writers earn enough money to make a living? It depends. The Department of Labor listed the average wage for full-time writers and authors as $60,250 in May 2015. For those who write advertising material, it was $53,530.

Writers who work for one publication or company are paid a fixed salary. Most of these employers also offer health care and paid time off for vacation or illness. These jobs are fairly stable. Other writers

WHAT IS AN ADVANCE?

Authors receive what is called an advance from a publisher before their book is published. It is an estimated percentage of what the book might earn after it goes on sale. Advances allow authors to have money while they spend time writing a book. Some famous authors are paid millions of dollars in advances. But most authors can expect to receive around $30,000 in advance when they sign with a major publisher.

Rick Riordan, author of the Percy Jackson series, received a $15,000 advance for his first book.

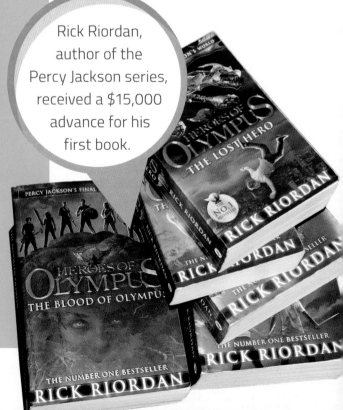

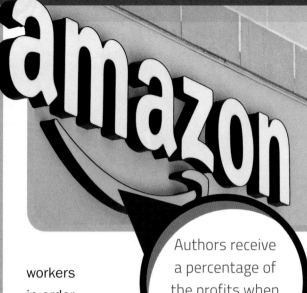

$19.5 million

Amount Jeff Kinney earned in one year from the sales of the Diary of a Wimpy Kid series.

- Writers who work for one company earn a fixed salary.
- Freelancing is exciting, but it can be hard to find steady work.
- Some writers get other jobs to help pay the bills.

Authors receive a percentage of the profits when their books are sold to Amazon.

do freelance work. These writers work for themselves. They choose which projects they want to work on. They create content for a variety of publications. Some earn an hourly wage. Others are paid by the word or by the article. Once the project is finished, the freelancer's work is done.

Working as a freelance writer is very rewarding. But it can be difficult to find steady work. Sometimes freelancers don't make enough money to support themselves or a family. Many get "day jobs" as teachers or office

workers in order to add to their income.

Authors receive a percentage of each book they sell. These percentages are called royalties. Royalty checks help authors pay for their daily living expenses. The rest of the money goes to publishers, agents, and bookstores or online retailers, such as Amazon.

THINK ABOUT IT

Discount retailers allow consumers to buy books at a reduced cost. This means publishers and authors receive less money. Should retailers be allowed to discount books? Why or why not?

How Are Speeches Written?

Lots of people need to give speeches as part of their jobs. The President of the United States gives the State of the Union address to members of Congress. The leader of a company presents new business ideas to board members. Actors give inspirational talks at charity events.

However, some of these people might not be great at writing. They might have trouble getting their thoughts

President Obama gives a speech at the United Nations.

22

Number of days it took to write the first draft of President Barack Obama's 2015 State of the Union address.

- Speechwriters create inspiring speeches for public speakers.
- Sometimes they work alone, but other times they work in teams.
- A speech needs lots of revising before it is ready to be presented.

Actors, such as Anne Hathaway, might use speechwriters at awards ceremonies.

across or telling an interesting story. That is where a speechwriter comes in.

Speechwriters take an individual or group of people's ideas and write a clear essay. They make sure the speech sounds interesting and inspiring when read out loud. They might spend many hours alone doing research for a speech. Or they might collaborate with members of a team.

Speechwriters should always check their work to make sure facts are correct.

Speechwriters usually write many drafts of a speech before reaching a final version. Speechwriters revise their work often. They take out paragraphs and rearrange sentences. Many speechwriters read what they have written out loud to see if it makes sense. Writing speeches is time consuming. But it is a job that helps others look and sound their best.

What Is an Editor?

Editors have one of the most important jobs in the writing world. They help make a writer's work the best it can be. Some editors help authors answer questions about the whole book, such as whether the plot makes sense. These editors help writers develop ideas into a manuscript. Developmental editors also help make sure readers will not be confused by an author's words or style.

Copyeditors work on a more technical level. They correct spelling, grammar, and punctuation errors. For nonfiction writing, some copyeditors also check facts to make sure they are correct.

Editors used to use red pencils to mark their edits on paper.

117,200
Number of editors working in the United States in 2014.

- Editors review and correct documents for content, style, and grammar.
- There are many types of editors.
- Editors can find work outside of publishing.
- Most companies prefer editors with a college degree.

Many editors use laptops to take work with them wherever they go.

Editors work in publishing houses or on their own. They work on many different manuscripts. Other editors manage sections of magazines, newspapers, or online publications. They hire freelance writers to contribute articles about food, local events, sports, or other subjects.

But editing jobs are not found only in publishing. Businesses hire editors in their marketing or communications departments, too. These editors review newsletters, write press releases, and create content for websites.

Most employers look for editors with a college degree in English, communications, or journalism. They also prefer candidates who understand how to use the latest technology.

Are Agents Necessary?

Tens of thousands of books are published every year in the United States. There are also hundreds of publishing companies. How do writers choose which publishers to send their manuscripts to? How do publishers decide which books might be good enough to sell? There's a person who takes care of both jobs.

A literary agent helps authors work with publishers. Agents contact publishers with manuscripts and help authors get book deals. Agents also help authors by discussing

Authors looking to publish with Penguin Random House will have better luck using an agent.

96

Percent of unpublished manuscripts that are rejected by literary agents.

- Literary agents work with authors and publishers to find the best match.
- Most agents specialize in one or two genres.
- Agents help authors understand the business side of contracts.
- Manuscripts from new authors are put in the slush pile.

John Green, author of *The Fault in Our Stars*, uses Writers House agency.

their contracts. Publishers work with agents to agree on how big an author's advance will be. Every agent specializes in one or a few genres, such as science fiction or health and wellness books.

Agents typically receive many unpublished manuscripts every day. Manuscripts from brand-new authors are put in what is called a slush pile. Sometimes manuscripts can sit in the slush pile for a year or longer before an agent reads it.

Not all writers use an agent to get published. Some send their work directly to editors at various publishing houses. But most writers find agents to be quite helpful. New writers can rely on agents to help them understand the publishing process.

Why Is Plagiarism Bad?

Coming up with an original idea is hard. Finding new and interesting ways to explain facts or stories is even harder. But the worst thing a writer can do is plagiarize. Why? Taking ownership of someone else's words or ideas is morally wrong. Copying another writer's work can also be copyright infringement, which is illegal.

Plagiarism can take many forms. If someone takes information from another book and does not give the author credit, that is plagiarism. If a student copies and pastes even one sentence from a website, that is plagiarism.

Harvard University expelled approximately 70 students in 2013 for plagiarism.

32

Percent of high school students who admitted to plagiarizing in 2012.

- Plagiarism means stealing another person's words or ideas.
- Copying and pasting from any source is plagiarism.
- Students can get kicked out of school for plagiarism.
- Plagiarists can be sued by other writers.

Both schools and businesses consider plagiarism to be stealing. No matter what the circumstances, the punishment for plagiarism can be severe. A student who plagiarizes might get kicked out of school. An employee who plagiarizes could get fired. Some authors who have plagiarized have been sued for large amounts of money.

Writers who are caught plagiarizing are often excluded by other writers. Writers who copy large amounts of text protected by copyright can be ordered to pay a large fine or thrown in jail.

HOW JAYSON BLAIR RUINED HIS CAREER

Jayson Blair was once a star reporter. He wrote articles for the *New York Times*. But in 2003, his boss discovered that Blair had been lying for years. Blair had made up quotes from fake sources. He had plagiarized articles from other newspapers. Blair even claimed he traveled to certain places to conduct interviews when he did not. When the truth was discovered, Blair was fired. At 27, his career as a journalist was over.

Almost half the articles Jayson Blair wrote during his last six months at the *New York Times* were either plagiarized or inaccurate.

Why Are Writers Important?

Why do words matter? That is a hard question to answer. But words have the power to transform lives.

Consider Martin Luther King Jr. He was a leader in the Civil Rights Movement during the 1960s. But he was also a writer. The speeches he wrote and delivered affected thousands of people. His words helped a generation peacefully demand equal rights for minorities.

Rachel Carson specialized in science writing. In 1962, she published *Silent Spring*. It discussed the dangers of using toxic chemicals in nature. The book was so well written that it started the environmental movement.

J. K. Rowling began writing bits of stories on napkins in cafés. But her series about a young wizard named

Rachel Carson was a marine biologist before becoming a writer.

Harry Potter inspired millions of kids and adults around the world to read more.

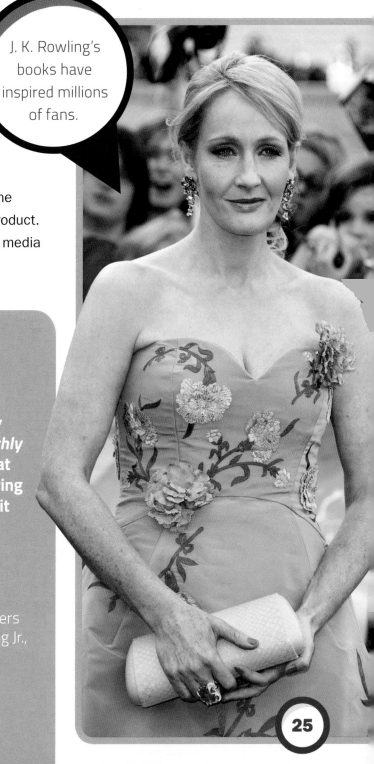

J. K. Rowling's books have inspired millions of fans.

Writing can spark change in smaller ways, too. An advertisement can spread the word about a healthy new product. Something written on social media can go viral.

8.3 million

Number of *Harry Potter and the Deathly Hallows* copies that were purchased during the first 24 hours it was on sale.

- Words and writing can change lives for the better.
- Some important writers are Martin Luther King Jr., Rachel Carson, and J. K. Rowling.
- Writing can make an impact in big and small ways.

Is Becoming a Writer Right for You?

When considering whether to become a writer, there are lots of things to think about. No two writers are exactly the same. But there are some general traits many writers have in common.

Most writers like to read. By reading what others have written, writers can learn how to be better writers. Reading also helps writers boost their vocabulary and understand the difference between genres.

A love for telling stories is key for becoming a writer—both true stories and fictional ones. The ability to transform complicated information into ideas that are easy to understand is also important. Creativity is a must.

A writer should also feel comfortable being alone. Working on a project, especially a book, often means long hours in front of a computer. Revising a manuscript or article

Revising a manuscript can take just as long as writing a first draft.

takes concentration. Sometimes people or background noise can be distracting.

Finally, writers have to learn how to not take rejection or criticism personally. Stephen King's first big novel was rejected 30 times. One publisher told J. K. Rowling that she needed to take a writing class. Writers deal with a lot of rejection. But those who keep trying will often succeed.

In 2000, Stephen King published *On Writing*, which contains advice for new writers.

431,626
Number of people who participated in National Novel Writing Month in 2015.

- Writers often enjoy reading.
- Writing takes creativity and focus.
- A writer must learn how to deal with rejection and criticism.

THINK ABOUT IT

Do you think becoming a writer is a good career choice for you? Why or why not? What type of writing do you think would fit your personality best?

Other Jobs to Consider

Ghostwriter

Description: Write and publish books or articles under someone else's name, such as a celebrity

Training/Education: Bachelor's degree

Outlook: Steady

Average salary: $60,250

Screenwriter

Description: Write scripts for television shows or movies

Training/Education: No formal education needed, but a bachelor's degree is often helpful

Outlook: Steady

Average Salary: $60,250

Marketing Manager

Description: Write press releases, brochures, and e-newsletters to promote a product or idea
Training/Education: Bachelor's degree
Outlook: Growing
Average salary: $124,850

Technical Writer

Description: Write instruction manuals, articles, and how-to guides to explain complicated technical information
Training/Education: Bachelor's degree or work experience in a related field
Outlook: Growing
Average salary: $70,240

Glossary

blog
A regularly updated web page that is usually run by one person or a small group.

collaborate
Work together.

employer
A person or company who hires someone to do a job.

fiction
A type of literature that is made up.

freelancers
Writers who work for themselves and submit work to many publications or companies.

genre
A type or category of literature, such as fiction, mystery, or fantasy.

internships
Temporary positions that focus on job training.

manuscripts
Drafts of a book.

marketing
The act of promoting or selling products or ideas; often a department in a company.

plagiarize
The act of taking someone's ideas or words and claiming them as your own.

royalties
Sums of money paid to authors according to the number of books sold.

traits
Qualities or characteristics that define a personality or person.

For More Information

Books

Anderson, Jennifer Joline. *Writing Fantastic Fiction*. Minneapolis: Lerner Publications, 2016.

Hambleton, Vicki, and Cathleen Greenwood. *So, You Want to Be a Writer? How to Write, Get Published, and Maybe Even Make It Big!* New York: Aladdin/Beyond Words, 2012.

Mazer, Anne, and Ellen Potter. *Spilling Ink: A Young Writer's Handbook*. New York: Roaring Brook Press, 2010.

Visit 12StoryLibrary.com

Scan the code or use your school's login at **12StoryLibrary.com** for recent updates about this topic and a full digital version of this book. Enjoy free access to:

- Digital ebook
- Breaking news updates
- Live content feeds
- Videos, interactive maps, and graphics
- Additional web resources

Note to educators: Visit 12StoryLibrary.com/register to sign up for free premium website access. Enjoy live content plus a full digital version of every 12-Story Library book you own for every student at your school.

Index

About the Author

Alexis Burling makes her living as a writer and book critic. She has written dozens of articles and books for young readers on a variety of topics ranging from current events and famous people, nutrition and fitness, relationships and cooking.

READ MORE FROM 12-STORY LIBRARY

Every 12-Story Library book is available in many formats. For more information, visit 12StoryLibrary.com.